Cheeky Jokes

for kids

First published in Great Britain 1988 by Ward Lock Limited,

This edition published 2004 by Bounty Books,
a division of Octopus Publishing Group Ltd,
2-4 Heron Quays, London E14 4JP
Reprinted 2004

ISBN 0 7537 0882 5

Printed and Bound in China

Cheeky Jokes
for kids

Bounty
Books

Alec: 'When I grow up I want to be a millionaire. I'll own a big mansion without any bathrooms.'
John: 'Why no bathrooms?'
Alec: 'Because I want to be filthy rich!'

Mum: 'Did you thank Mrs Smith for inviting you to the party?'
Alec: 'No – the boy before me thanked her.'

'How can you make a tall man short?'
   'Ask him to lend you all his money.'

Alec: 'A friend of mine was on a coconut diet.'
John: 'How much weight did he lose'
Alec: 'None, but you should see him climb trees!'

Doctor, doctor, my son has just swallowed a bullet. What should I do?'

'To begin with, don't point him at me!'

Young sister: 'Is it good manners to eat chicken with your fingers?'
Alec: 'No, you should eat your fingers separately.'

Dad: 'How can you say that a forger is a good person?'
Alec: 'Because he is always writing wrongs!'

Teacher: 'I asked everyone in the classroom to draw a ring. Why did you draw a square?'
Alec: 'This square is a ring - a boxing ring!'

Uncle: 'I made two trips across the Atlantic and never took a bath.'
Alec: 'I'd say that makes you a dirty double crosser!'

Mum: 'My friend thinks she has the face of a twenty-year-old girl.'
Alec: 'Well she'd better give it back - she's making it all wrinkled!'

Friend: 'What was Snow White's brother's name?'
Alec: 'Egg White! Get the yolk?'

'There are a lot of fans at his show.'
    'They probably can't afford air-conditioning!'

Alec: 'This soup is awful!'
Waiter: 'Why do you say that?'
Alec: 'A little swallow told me!'

Friend: 'I can lie in bed and watch the sun rise.'
Alec: 'So what? I can sit on a chair and watch the kitchen sink!'

'Can you stretch the music out a bit longer?'
    'Sorry, sir, but this is a dance band, not a rubber band!'

Dentist: 'What kind of filling do you want me to put in your mouth?'
Alec: 'Chocolate fudge would be nice!'

'Waiter, what's this fly doing in my soup?'
    'It looks like the backstroke to me, sir!'

Aunt: 'When do you like school best?'
Alec: 'When it's closed!'

Girlfriend: 'Did you notice how the opera singer's voice filled the hall?'
Alec: 'Yes. I also noticed how a lot of people left to make room for it!'

Alec: 'A dog just bit me on my ankle.'
Doctor: 'Did you put anything on it?'
Alec: 'No, he liked it just as it was!'

Teacher: 'If I had ten apples in one hand and twelve apples in the other hand, what would I have?'
Alec: 'The biggest hands anyone's ever seen!'

Landowner: 'You are not allowed to fish here.'
Alec: 'I'm not fishing, I'm just giving my pet worm a bath!'

Girlfriend: 'Did your watch stop when you dropped it on the floor?'
Alec: 'Of course it did! Why, did you think it would go right through the ground?'

Friend: 'So your dad collects fleas. What does your mum do?'
Alec: 'Scratch!'

WORM SOAP

'Why did your dad set light to his coat?'
  The shop told him it was a blazer!'

Alec: 'What does the X-ray of my brain show?'
Doctor: 'Nothing!'

John: 'The ointment the doctor gave me makes my hands smart.'
Alec: 'Then I suggest you rub some on your head!'

Girlfriend: 'I've just swallowed a roll of film.'
Alec: 'Don't worry, nothing serious can develop!'

Friend: 'Where do fleas go in winter?'
Alec: 'Search me!'

Music teacher: 'Can you sing tenor?'
Alec: 'I would if I could, but I don't know the words!'

Mother: 'Wash your hands, your piano teacher will soon be here.'
Alec: 'No problem! I'll only play on the black notes!'

Teacher: 'Why are the Middle Ages called the Dark Ages?'
Alec: 'That's easy - because there were so many knights in them!'

'Why are you cleaning up the spilled soup with your cake?'
    'It's a sponge cake!'

Mum: 'The florist has two children.'
Alec: 'I know! One is a budding genius and the other is a blooming idiot!'

'What happened to the couple who met in a revolving door?'
    'They're still going around together!'

Alec: 'I can lift an elephant with one hand!'
Friend: 'That's impossible!'
Alec: 'No it's not. Find me an elephant that has one hand and I'll prove it to you!'

Mum: 'How did you get that lump on your nose?'
Alec: 'I bent down to smell a brose.'
Mum: 'It's not a brose, it's a rose. There's no B is rose.'
Alec: 'There was in this one!'

Mother: 'Did you give the goldfish some fresh water?'
Alec: 'No, they haven't drunk the water I gave them yesterday!'

Girlfriend: 'Now we've decided to get married, I hope you will give me a ring.'
Alec: 'Of course I will. What's your number?'

'You say your girlfriend fell overboard in shark-infested waters, but the sharks didn't bother her?'
'That's right. They were *man*-eating sharks.'

'Waiter, will my hamburger be long?'
'No, sir. It will be round.'

DID I HEAR HAMBURGER?

Teacher: 'Spell mouse.'
Alec: 'M-O-U-S.'
Teacher: 'But what's on the end of it?'
Alec: 'A tail!'

'Where was Queen Victoria going when she was in her 39th year?'
    'Into her 40th!'

Sister: 'I heard a loud noise this morning.'
Alec: 'It must have been the crack of dawn!'

'Doctor, doctor, I have a terrible problem. Can you help me out?'
    'Of course! Which way did you come in?'

Alec: 'Are waiters supposed to be tipped?'
Waiter: 'Of course.'
Alec: 'Good, then you can tip me, I've been waiting for service for twenty minutes!'

Teacher: 'What is a prickly pear?'
Alec: 'That's easy! Two porcupines.'

Teacher: 'Where was the Magna Carta signed?'
Alec: 'At the bottom. Where else?'

'Why do you say that Rome must have been built at night?'
    'Because I keep hearing people say it wasn't built in a day!'

Teacher: 'Where are the kings and queens of Great Britain usually crowned?'
Alec: 'On the head, of course!'

'How many people work in your office?'
'About half of them!'

Teacher: 'The ruler of Russia was called the Czar and his wife was the Czarina. What were their children called?
Alec: 'Czardines?'

Teacher: 'Why does the Statue of Liberty stand in New York Harbour?'
Alec: 'Because it can't sit down!'

Mother: 'You've put your shoes on the wrong feet.'
Alec: 'But these are the only feet I have!'

'Why are you scratching yourself?'
    'Because nobody else knows exactly where I itch!'

Waiter: 'How did you find your steak, sir?'
Alec: 'I looked under a chip - and there it was!'

'I can't seem to fall asleep at night.'
    'Try sleeping by the edge of the bed. You'll soon drop off!'

Dad: 'How were the exam questions?'
Alec: 'Fine. It was the answers I had trouble with!'

Alec: 'Would you punish a kid for something he didn't do?'
Teacher: 'Of course not!'
Alec: 'Good. I didn't do my homework!'

Teacher: 'How can you prove the world is round?'
Alec: 'I never claimed it was, sir.'

Teacher: 'What month has 28 days?'
Alec: 'All of them!'

Captain: 'Why didn't you try to stop the ball?'
Goalie: 'I thought that was what the net was for!'

'Would you like a pocket calculator for Christmas?'

'Not really. I already know how many pockets I have.'

Does this band take requests?'
    'Certainly.'
'In that case, I request they stop playing!'

Teacher: 'Name the four seasons.'
Alec: 'Salt, pepper, vinegar and mustard!'

'My baby's been walking since he was nine months old.'
    'Really? He must be very tired!'

Judge: 'Haven't you been up before me before?'
Prisoner: 'I'm not sure. What time do you usually get up?'

Alec: 'Do you have a good memory for faces?'
Dad: 'Yes, why?
Alec: 'I've just broken your shaving mirror!'

Sergeant: 'What were you before you joined the army?'
New recruit: 'Happy!'

Teacher: 'If you found 50p in one pocket and 75p in the other pocket, what would you have?'
Alec: 'Somebody else's trousers!'

Alec: 'My dad just bought a baby car.'
Friend: 'What do you mean?'
Alec: 'It won't go anywhere without a rattle!'

Alec: 'Do you have holes in your trousers?'
Friend: 'Of course I don't!'
Alec: 'Then how do you get your legs through?'

Mum: 'Why do you eat everything with your knife?'
Alec: 'My fork leaks!'

Alec: 'When my fingers heal, will I be able to play the piano?'
Doctor: 'Of course.'
Alec: 'Great! I never could before!'

Teacher: 'To what family does the rhinoceros belong?'
Alec: 'I don't know, but I'm sure it's no family in our street!'

'Is your horse well-behaved?'
    'Yes. When we come to a fence he stops and lets me go over first!'

Alec: 'What would you like for Christmas?'
Sister: 'Make it a surprise.'
Alec: 'Right. BOO!'

'I suppose this horrible picture is what you call modern art?'

'No, it's a mirror!'

Uncle: 'What are you going to give your sister for Christmas?'
Alec: 'I'm not sure. Last year I gave her measles!'

Alec: 'Do you believe in free speech?'
Neighbour: 'Of course.'
Alec: 'Good, because I need to borrow your phone to make a long-distance call.'

Teacher: 'How many fingers do you have?'
Alec: 'Ten.'
Teacher: 'And if you lost three of them, what would you have?'
Alec: 'No more piano lessons!'

'Why is your brother crying?'
    'Because I won't give him my piece of cake.'
'What about his own piece of cake?'
    'He cried when I ate that too!'

Friend: 'The police are looking for a man with one eye called Sam.'
Alec: 'What's his other eye called?'

Judge: 'Order, order in the courtroom!'
Alec: 'I'll have fish and chips with pickles, followed by ice cream, please!'

Friend: 'Do you always remember to say a prayer before dinner?'
Alec: 'There's no need. My mum is a good cook.'

'What's the weather like?'
'I don't know. It's too cloudy to see.'

Angry man: 'I'll teach you to throw stones at my greenhouse!'
Alec: 'I wish you would. I keep missing it!'

Did you hear the one about the man who invented a comb for bald men? It had no teeth!

'Doctor, can you give me something for my liver?'
'How about some onions?'

'Why does your dad work at the bread factory?'
'He kneads the dough!'

Alec: 'I'm glad you don't have a duel personality.'
Sheila: 'Why?'
Alec: 'The one you have is bad enough!'

John: 'Did you hear the joke about dustmen?'
Alec: 'Don't bother to tell it, it's probably just a load of rubbish!'

Ivan: 'Why do some women put rollers in their hair before they go to sleep?'
Alec: 'So they'll wake up *curly* in the morning!'

Alec: 'Will this bus take me to London?'
Bus driver: 'Which part?'
Alec: 'All of me, of course!'

Alec said to Ivan, 'You are my friend and I'd like to pay you a compliment - but I can't think of one!'

John: 'I'd like to be a litter collector. Do you think I need some special training?'
Alec: 'No, you'll pick it up as you go along.'

John: 'How much do you like me?'
Alec: 'As friends go, you're fine. And the sooner you go, the better!'

Alec told Harry, 'Your brain is the weakest part of your body, but at least it's protected by the strongest part - your thick skull!'

'I keep talking to myself.'
     'No wonder. No one else would listen to you!'

Friend: 'Girls always fall in love with me at first sight.'
Alec: 'I know. It's when they take a second look that they can't stand you!'

'Every time I pass a girl she sighs.'
     'With relief!'

'Craig is good at everything he does.'
    'Yes, that's probably because he never does anything!'

Trudy: 'I was selected by a computer as an ideal girlfriend.'
Alec: 'Who wants to be a computer's girlfriend?'

'There's a twig in my soup!'
    'Call the branch manager!'

'Girls whisper that they love me.'
'Of course they do. They would never admit it out loud!'

Certain members of an orchestra can never be trusted - the fiddlers!

'What's the best way to keep water out of your house?'
'Don't pay the water rates!'

Alec: 'Do you know what the Eskimo girl did to her boyfriend?'
John: 'What?'
Alec: 'She gave him the cold shoulder!'

Alec: 'Did you hear the joke about the length of rope?'
Andrea: 'No.'
Alec: 'Skip it!'

Paul: 'I have a very clear mind.'
Alex: 'That's because it's empty!'

'This comedian is too dumb to be funny. In fact I don't think he could even entertain a thought!'

'*I'm going to mend my bad ways.*'
'You keep saying that, but the stitches are always breaking!'

'*I do lots of exercise.*'
'Yes, I can tell. You're certainly long-winded!'

'*How do fishermen make their nets?*'
'They take lots of holes and join them together!'

'*In what country do people always want to eat?*'
'In Hungary!'

Ivan: 'What do you call a butcher's boy?'
Alex: 'A chop assistant!'

'What did the knight in armour say when the king gave him a medal?'
    'You can't pin that on me!'

Mum: 'Shall I put the kettle on?'
Alex: 'Don't bother, I think the dress you're wearing looks better!'

'His head was so thick, when he joined the army, they told him he didn't need to wear a helmet!

Neighbour: 'How did you like the food?'
Alex: 'It was a real *swill* dinner!'

'I want a double portion of chips.'
'Isn't that expensive?'
'No, but it is expansive!'

Gail: 'Does your mum have an automatic dishwasher?'
Alec: 'Yes, my dad!'

Barbara: 'I'm not very smart. I don't think I could ever get a job.'
Alec: 'You could always be a ventriloquist's dummy!'

Alec: 'My dad was on a plane that had engine trouble.'
Bill: 'What did he do?'
Alec: 'He offered to get out and push!'

'Do you like your teacher?'
    'I can't complain. In fact, I wouldn't dare!'

'I don't think I could ever marry a woman who was stupid enough to want to marry me!'

'I always like to think the best of people. That's why I think of you as an idiot!'

'Do you have trouble making decisions?'
    'Um, well - yes and no!'

'I wonder what my I.Q. is?'
    'Don't worry about it. It's nothing!'

'My dad wants to work badly - and Mum says he usually does!

'What a crybaby!'
    'Yes, he's what you might call a regular Prince of Wails!'

Sue: 'How do you keep an idiot waiting?'
Alec: 'I'll tell you tomorrow!'

Friend: 'My dad just bought me a wooden engine with wooden wheels.'
Alec: 'I bet it wooden go!'

Little sister: 'Why do cows wear bells?'
Alec: 'Because their horns don't work!'

John: 'I've heard that Alaskan dogs can run the fastest.'
Alec: 'That's because the trees are so far apart!'

THAT'S WHY I DON'T LIVE IN ALASKA!

'She's always talking with her mouth full - of words!

'It's very hard for Tom to eat anything.'
    'Why?'
'He hates to stop talking!'

'When he's talking, I always think of an explosion in a mine.'
    'Why?'
'Because there is a lot of noise coming out of a big hole!'

Bob: 'I hear your brother has a quick mind.'
Alec: 'Yes, a real *scheme* engine!'

'My brother is very superstitious. In a boxing ring, he always keeps a horseshoe in his glove.'

Sheila: 'Is your brother willing to do an honest day's work?'
Alec: 'Yes, but he wants an honest week's pay for it!'

'My brother has a great way of saving money. He forgets whom he borrowed it from!'

'When I lent my brother some money, he said he'd be everlastingly in my debt. And he was right!

'My brother fell in love with his wife the second time he met her. The first time he didn't know she was rich!

Girlfriend: 'Did he really marry her because her father left her a fortune?'
Alec: 'He denies it. He says he would have married her no matter who left her a fortune.'

'My brother is so crooked, he even has to screw his socks on!'

'My brother is the most highly suspected man in the community.'

'Your dad claims to be around 35.'
    'Yes, but he's been around it a few times!'

Friend: 'Is your mum one of those people who lies about her age?'
Alec: 'Not really. She says she's as old as my dad, then lies about his age!'

'Mum says she doesn't want any more candles on her birthday cake. On her last birthday, there were so many candles, it looked like a forest fire!'

'Mum is a very decisive person. When she reached 45, she definitely decided what she wanted to be - 29!'

'My sister isn't lying when she says she turned 23. She did - ten years ago!'

'How old do you think your neighbour is?'
　　'Well, his grandparents were called Adam and Eve!'

'It's not true that my uncle only sits in the armchair all day. Sometimes he lies on the sofa!'

'My uncle believes in a balanced diet. He always holds food in both hands!'

Friend: 'I work for your brother and I really admire and respect him.'
Alec: 'Of course you do. If you didn't, you would be fired!'

'When he loses to me in tennis, he always grips my hand and shakes it.'
'Yes, that's so you won't be able to use it properly next time!'

'How does you dad handle temptation?'
'Oh, he yields to it!'

Friend: 'Is your dad brave?'
Alec: 'Brave? Put it this way, when he goes to the doctor, he needs an anaesthetic to sit in the waiting room!'

'My dad bites his nails so much, his stomach needs a manicure!'

Friend: 'Is your dad a member of the local golf club?'

Alec: 'No, he would never join any club that would take someone like him as a member!'

'Sometimes my hand shakes so much, I can thread the needle of a sewing machine when it's running!'

Friend: 'Is it true that your friend Jim is a miracle worker?'

Alec: 'Yes, it's a miracle when he works!'

'My brother isn't very popular at work. The other workers complain that his snoring always disturbs them!'

'There's only one job that my brother would really like - tester in a mattress factory!'

'*Why did your brother learn to play the trombone?*'
    'It's the only instrument on which you can get anywhere by letting things slide.'

'At bedtime, my brother has his prayers printed and pasted on the wall because he's too lazy to read them. He just says, "Lord, please will you read them?"'

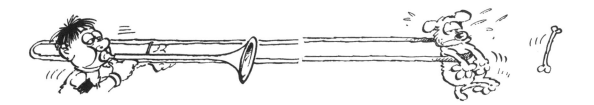

'There is one thing you can say for my brother. He always puts in a good day's work. The problem is, it takes him a fortnight to do it!'

'My brother has been fired for working eight hours and sleeping eight hours.'
    'What's wrong with that?'
'They are the same eight hours!'

'My brother gets his exercise by watching horror films. They make his flesh creep!'

'Doesn't Bill look tired?'
    'Yes. Last week he fell asleep while running for the bus!'

'*What did your dad say to your mum when he married her?*'
    'He said that a marriage and a career don't mix. Since then, he hasn't worked!'

'*My mum's hat is very becoming.*'
    'You mean it's becoming worn out!'

'*Did you notice that ugly thing growing on my brother's neck?*'
    'Yes, it's called his head!'

My brother is so dumb, that when he went to see a mind reader, he was only charged half price!'

'Many doctors have examined his head - but they can't find anything in it!'

'My sister says she has a mind of her own. But that's only because no one else would want it!'

I CAN SMELL SOMETHIN'

'I feel sorry for your poor little mind - all alone in a great big head!'

'Everyone in our family is hoping Tom will get ahead'
    'Yes, he looks funny with nothing on the top of his neck!'

'My dad says my mum is like a Greek statue - beautiful, but not all there!'

Friend: 'My brother often has something on his mind.'
Alec: 'Only when he wears a hat!'

He should be careful not to let his mind wander.
It's too weak to be let out alone!'

'When my brother moved up to the next class he
was so excited he cut himself shaving!

'They say that ignorance is bliss.'
     'Then you should be the happiest girl in the
world!'

Friend: 'What makes you think Timothy is dumb?'
Alec: 'He said he was working on a new invention - colour radio!'

'Why is she standing on her head?'
  'She's turning things over in her mind.'

Friend: 'My mum is always sunbathing.'
Alec: 'Perhaps she wants to be the toast of the town!'

Alec: 'There's no point telling you a joke with a double meaning.'
Friend: 'Why not?'
Alec:: 'You won't get either of them!'

'My friend is so dumb, he couldn't even spell
OTTO backwards!'

Friend: 'I just read that a woman gives birth to a
baby every minute.'
Alec: 'Someone should find her and stop her!'

'I want to live to 110.'
    'I know why. Very few people die after that
age!'

'Someone gave my dad an electric toothbrush, but he won't use it because he can't work out if his teeth are AC or DC!'

My brother is finding it difficult to find a girlfriend. He's looking for a woman who will love him as much as he does!

'I want you to accept my opinion for what it's worth.'
　　'In that case, you owe me 50p.

Friend: 'That new boy Peter really has staying power.'
Alec: 'I know. He never leaves!'

'*My dad is always welcome in the best homes.*'
    'Of course he is. He's a plumber!'

'He's not a very sincere person. In fact the only genuine thing about him is his false teeth!'

'*My brother has been at university for many years.*'
    'I know. I hear he has more degrees than a thermometer!'

'*Is your stomach O.K.?*'
    'Why do you ask?'
'*I just wanted to know if it was as sour as your face.*'

'*Dad keeps saying that Mum is very dear to him.*'
    'He means she costs him a fortune!'

'*You're only as old as you think.*'
    'In that case, you must be about three months.'

'*I never act stupid.*'
    'No, with you it's always the real thing.'

'Let's have an agreement. If you don't say anything, I won't listen!'

'*His thoughts are written all over his face.*'
    'Yes, he certainly has a blank expression.'

'*I'm thinking hard.*'
    'Don't you mean it's hard for you to think?'

'I'm going to the beauty parlour.'
  'I didn't know they could perform miracles!'

'Do you think she looks bad?'
  'She could look worse - if I had better eyesight!'

Neighbour: 'My son has had many requests.'
Alec: 'I know. But he insists on playing anyway!'

'Music has a terrible effect upon my friend. It makes her want to sing!'

George: 'My girlfriend is as pretty as a flower.'
Alec: 'A cauliflower!'

'I'm not saying she's not pretty, but if you pulled her pigtail she would say, "Oink, oink!"'

'I told my husband to tell me everything he knows.'
    'He must have been speechless!'

George: 'I think much faster than you.'
Alec: 'I can tell. You've stopped already!'

George: 'Let's play a game of wits.'
Alec: 'No, let's choose a game you can play too!'

Louise: 'I have a ready wit.'
Alec: 'Let me know when it's ready.'

'Does your husband have a happy home life?'
'It's hard to tell. He's never there.'

'My friend had her house built in a canyon with an echo. Now she can listen to herself talk without even speaking!'

'Look at my new baby brother. The stork brought him.'

 'He looks more like a seagull dropped him!'

Louise: 'I love nightlife...'
Alec: 'Owls, rodents...'

Alec: 'You would make a perfect - ''
Carol: 'Perfect what?'
Alec: 'Stranger!'

'My sister is always looking in a mirror.'
    'Not when she's backing out of a parking space!'

'My mum has never said an unkind word about anyone.'
    'That's because she only talks about herself!'

'My dad is happy we live in the machine age.'
    'That's because he thinks he's a big wheel.'

Geraldine: 'My dad suffers from migraine.'
Alec: 'That's probably because his halo is too tight!'

'Do you think he's conceited?'
    'Who else has a mirror on the bathroom ceiling so he can watch himself gargle?'

'I've often wondered why he never takes a shower.'
    'It's probably because the steam clouds the mirror, so he's unable to admire himself!'

'He's a real big gun in the office..'

'He should be careful - or they might fire him.'

'Just look at him. Isn't he a seedy character?'
'Seedy! Why, he trembles every time he passes a canary!'

'My boss was upset when I told him I was quitting my job next week.'
'He was probably hoping you would quit this week!'

'I've been staying awake at nights, trying to figure out a way to succeed.'
'You might be better off staying awake during the day!'

SO? – I CAN'T HELP BEING GOOD-LOOKING!

'Even when opportunity knocks, my neighbour complains about the noise!'

'My dad has his ups and downs.'
    'Does he? Mine just goes around in circles.'

'I'm now going out with a girl who's different to all the other girls.'
    'You bet she's different! She's the only girl in town who will go out with you!'

MY SOCK'S LEFT ME – I'M SO LONELY!!

'Nobody could call her a quitter.'
　　'Of course not. She's been fired from every job she's had!'

'My dad started at the bottom, and he enjoyed it so much he's stayed there ever since!'

Lenny: 'My dad took a test to find out what he was best suited for.'
Alec: 'I know. They discovered he was best suited for retirement!'

Brenda: 'My dad wanted to be a lawyer badly.'
Alec: 'Well he's certainly realized his ambition. He *is* a bad lawyer!'

'My sister is the only one I know who can speak five languages - and doesn't know how to say 'thank you' in any of them!'

Jim: 'Looks aren't everything.'
Alec: 'In your case they aren't anything!'

'He has a very sympathetic face.'
   'Yes, it gets everyone's sympathy!'

'I know someone who is so ugly, he has to sneak up on the mirror to shave!'

'He looks much better without my glasses!'

'What do you think of Jim's looks?'
    'I don't mind him looking. It's his face I can't stand!'

'Jim was a war baby.'
    'I know. His parents took one look at him and started fighting!'

'Alec hates flying. He says he can never walk out of a boring movie!'

'Mum always puts a little oil on her skin at night.'
    'That's why she *slides* out of bed in the morning!'

Caroline: 'Have you noticed that Jack has a nasty blemish between his ears?'
Alec: 'Yes, it's called his face!'

Caroline: 'I hear Susan appeared in a beauty contest and got several offers.'
Alec: 'Yes, they were all from plastic surgeons!'

'Mum said I'm like an angel that fell from the sky.'
'It's too bad you fell on your face!'

'His teeth are all his own.'
'You mean he's finished paying for them at last?'

'Every so often Dave puts on a mud pack.'
'Does it help?'
'It improves his looks for a few days, but then the mud falls off!'

'My gran's skin is nearly as smooth as a prune!'

'I know someone who has such a big mouth, she can sing a duet all by herself! In fact when she yawns, you can't see her ears!'

'Still, she has a pretty head on her shoulders.'
    'Perhaps, but it would be better if there was a neck in between.'

'Dad has a Roman nose.'
    'Yes, it roams all over his face!'

GRRR - US TEETH SHOULD STICK TOGETHER!

'Dad goes to the dentist twice a year - once for each tooth!'

'Dad's very clean.'
    'Yes, he takes a bath once a month whether he needs one or not!'

Caroline: 'My neighbour is looking quite old.'
Alec: 'Quite? He has so many wrinkles on his forehead, he has to screw on his hat!'

'My uncle is so bald, you can't look at him in a bright light without wearing sunglasses!'

'My friend is so short-sighted, he once picked up a poisonous snake to hit a stick!'

Girlfriend: 'Is it true that carrots improve your vision?'
Alec: 'Well, have you ever seen a rabbit wearing glasses?'

Girlfriend: 'Did you know that it takes three sheep to knit a sweater?'
Alec: 'Really? I didn't even know sheep could knit!'

Girlfriend: 'That jumper doesn't do much for Mary, does it?'
Alec: 'Put it this way - I preferred it when it was still on the sheep!'

'He's so skinny, when he's drinking tomato juice he looks like a thermometer!'

'*Martin says he's a light eater.*'
　　'He is. As soon as it's light outside, he starts eating!'

'*Martin insists that he eats like a bird.*'
　　'Yes, a *vulture*!'

'*I'm really watching my weight.*'
　　'Watching it go up, you mean!'

'I once had a million dollar figure - but then inflation set in!'

'*Danny is such a gossip, but he looks very unhappy.*'
　　'That's because he only has one mouth!'

'My dad has put on a lot of weight. His belly is so big, he says he can now take a shower without getting his feet wet!'

'For years she's been planning a runaway marriage with her boyfriend. But every time the big day arrives, he runs away!'

John: 'Girls don't call me names!'
Alec: 'They don't call you at all!'

'She was two-thirds married once.'
  'What do you mean?'
'Well, she was there, the minister was there - but the groom didn't show up!'

'Bob has a leaning towards blondes.'
  'I know, but they keep pushing him away!'

'Any girl that goes out with him must appreciate the simpler things in life.'

'His girlfriend returned all his letters.'
   'I bet she marked them *2nd Class Male*.'

'Bill has a duel personality.'
   'Yeah, Dr Heckle and Mr Snide.'

'Tom hasn't been himself lately.'
   'I've noticed the improvement!'

'Do you think he has many faults?'
   'Only two. What he says - and what he does!'

'People like Harry don't grow on trees.'
   'I know. They swing from them!'

'People don't seem to like Jack very much.'
   'No. If he ever needs a friend, he'll have to buy a dog!

'He's a man of many parts.'
   'Yes, but it was a terrible assembly job.'

Bob: 'I hear you live on the 15th floor of a high-rise block. Do you have a good view?'
Alec: 'Yes, on a clear day I can see the ground!'

'He thinks everyone worships the ground he crawled out of!'

'He's the kind of man who could give a headache to an aspirin!'

John: 'My uncle says that when he dies, he wants to be buried face-down.'
Alec: 'Why?'
John: 'So he'll see where he's going!'

John: 'I heard your sister doesn't care for a man's company.'
Alec: 'Not unless he owns it!'

'Alec is so afraid of flying, he feels sick just licking an airmail stamp!'

Little sister: 'How do you become an airline pilot?'
Alec: 'You start at the bottom - and work your way up!'

'*John took Sue to one of the best restaurants.*'
    'Yes, but he didn't take her in!'

'*I'm told she buys all her jewellry from a famous millionaire.*'
    'Yes, Woolworth!'

'*She wears her wedding ring on the wrong finger.*'
    'She probably feels she married the wrong man!'

'The way my dad moans and groans when he gets even a slight cold, you can't decide whether to call the doctor or a drama critic!'

'I hear Dan's very highly strung.'
    'He's so highly strung I keep telling him to join a circus!'

John: 'Edward was born with a silver spoon in his mouth.'
Alec: 'Funny. All the other kids have tongues!'

'Alan comes up with an answer for every problem.'
    'Yes, but it's always wrong!'

'He's very dependable.'
    'Yes, you can always depend on him to do the wrong thing!'

'I saved for years to buy an unbreakable, waterproof, shockproof watch.'

'How do you like it?'
'I don't know, I lost it!'

'Terry is so dumb. He must have been practising for ages. No one can be that good at it by accident!

'He never hurts people's feelings.'
'Not unintentionally, anyway.'

OH YEAH!

John: 'Ben is a man with polish.'
Alec: 'Yes, but only on his shoes!'

John: 'At the restaurant, her table is always reserved.'
Alec: 'Too bad she isn't.'

'I've always thought of Jim as a true sportsman.'
    'I know what you mean. When he spots an empty seat on a train, he points it out to a passenger, then races them for it!'

'*Why does Anne prefer matches to a lighter?*'
'You can't pick your teeth with a lighter.'

'*I've heard she's a very economical person.*'
'Yes, she likes to save on soap and water!'

'I think Michael's a garbage collector. He has that certain air about him.'

'*I was told he was bitten by a rattlesnake.*'
'Yes. It was a terrible sight to watch that poor little snake curl up and die!'

'*Susan always thinks twice before speaking.*'
　　'Yes, so she can think up something really nasty!'

'When it comes to helping others, she'll stop at nothing!'

Bob: 'Well, as far as I'm concerned, a friend in need is -'
Alec: 'A friend to steer clear of!'

'You're so cold-blooded, if a mosquito bit you it would die of pneumonia!'

'*Peter reminds me of an accordion player.*'
   'Why?'
'*Because he plays both ends against the middle!*'

'*Why do they call Pat an after-dinner speaker?*'
   'Because every time she speaks to a man she's after a dinner!'

'*Why do they call her angel?*'
   'Because she's always harping on about things!'

'Why do they call Paul 'bean'?'
    'Because all the girls string him along!'

'Why do they call Janet a business woman?'
    'Because her nose is always in everybody's business!'

'Why do they call Chris caterpillar?'
    'Because he's got where he is by crawling!'

'Why do they call Fred 'Cliff'?'
    'Because he's just a big bluff!'

'Why didn't you come to school yesterday?'
    'I was sick - sick of school!'

John: 'What's your sister going to be when she grows up?'
Alec: 'An old lady!'

Teacher: 'Classes start at 8.45.'
Alec: 'O.K., but if I'm not here you have my permission to start without me.'

Father: 'I see you got a D for conduct but an A for courtesy, How is that possible?'
Alec: 'Well, whenever I'm rude to someone I say sorry.'

Alec handed in his exam paper and said, 'You'll find that my answers are a good indication of your ability as a teacher.'

'I thought you said I'd have a choice of greens, but I can only see one type of vegetable.'
    'The choice is: take it or leave it!'

Alec: 'Sometimes I really like my teacher.'
John: 'When's that?'
Alec: 'When she's sick and has to stay at home!'

'Wendy is a naturally talented cello player.'
    'I can tell that by her bow legs!'

'What's a tuba?'
    'It comes between a oneba and a threeba!'

Burt: 'Someone stole our upright piano.'
Alec: 'That's downright disgraceful!'

Alec: 'I'm very tired. I was up until twelve doing my homework.'
John: 'What time did you start?'
Alec: 'Eleven fifty-five.'

'Our teacher can do bird imitations.'
   'I know. She watches me like a hawk!'

'You're pretty dirty, Alec.'
   'I'm even prettier when I'm clean.'

Teacher: 'What do French children say when they've been served a school lunch?'
Alec: 'MERCY!'

Teacher: 'What happens to gold when it's exposed to the air?'
Alec: 'It's probably stolen!'

Teacher: 'Who can name a deadly poison?'
Alec: 'Aviation. One drop and you're dead!'

Alec: 'I have almost 3000 bones in my body.'
Teacher: 'You know that's not possible.'
Alec: 'Yes it is. I had a can of sardines for lunch!'

Teacher: 'Why don't you write more clearly?'
Alec: 'Then you'd see that I can't spell!'

'Why are you so late for school?'
    'I had to say goodbye to my pets.'
'But you are two hours late!'
    'I know, but I just got an ant farm!'

Alec: 'This restaurant must have a very clean kitchen.'
Waiter: 'Thank you. Why do you say that?'
Alec: 'Everything tastes of soap!'

'I didn't come here to be insulted.'
    'Where do you usually go?'

GOODBYE GOODBYE GOODBYE GOODBYE GOODBYE GOODBYE

Friend: 'I don't think the photo you took of me does me justice.'
Alec: 'You don't want justice, you want mercy!'

Sue: 'Some boys think I'm pretty and some boys think I'm ugly. What do you think?'
Jane: 'A bit of both - pretty ugly!'

Alec says that Harry should be an organist because he has so many pipe dreams!

Auntie: 'Do you like my dress? It's over 100 years old, you know!'
Alec: 'Did you make it yourself?'

Friend: 'I've got a cold in my head. How can I stop it going to my chest?'
Alec: 'Have you tried tying a knot in your neck?'

Friend: 'That girl looks like Helen Green.'
Alec: 'She looks even worse in red!'

'Why do you keep telling everyone I'm an idiot?'
  'Surely you're not trying to keep it a secret!'

'In the park I was surrounded by lions.'
   'Lions in the park?'
'That's right, dandelions.'

Dad: 'Did you get my golf gear?'
Alec: 'Yes, here's your map, compass, emergency rations...'

Friend: 'Is that right - your dad got a birdie on the 4th?'
Alec: 'Yes, a poor little sparrow!'

Girlfriend: 'What's a caddie?'
Alec: 'Someone who follows his work schedule to a tee!'

Golfer: 'I'd move heaven and earth to break 100.'
Alec: 'Concentrate on heaven - you've already moved enough earth!'

Golfer: 'Do you like my game?'
Alec: 'Not bad, but I still prefer golf!'

BOY - THIS TASTES BETTER THAN BONES

'A tuba is a musical instrument.'
   'Not when it's a tube of toothpaste!'

Alec: 'Will you still love me when I'm old and ugly?'
Girlfriend: 'Of course I do!'

Alec: 'I'm the most advanced kid in the class!'
Mum: 'Really?'
Alec: 'Yes, I sit at the front.'

Friend: 'What does your father do?'
Alec: 'He's a government artist.'
Friend: 'What does he draw?'
Alec: 'The dole!'

Sister: 'For my birthday I'd like a dress to match my eyes.'
Alec: 'Where can I buy a bloodshot dress?'

Sister: 'There's a man at the door collecting for old people.'
Alec: 'Well he's not having Granny!'

Sue: 'Do you think it will rain today?'
Alec: 'I guess it all depends on the weather.'

Alec: 'I can't leave you.'
Girlfriend: 'Do you love me so much?'
Alec: 'It's not that. You're standing on my shoelace!'

Girlfriend: 'I'm the teacher's pet.'
Alec: 'Can't she afford a cat?'

Friend: 'Every time I feel down in the dumps I buy myself a new suit.'
Alec: 'So that's where you get your clothes!'

Friend: 'My girlfriend's really smart. She has brains enough for two.'
Alec: 'Sounds like the right girl for you!'

Teacher: 'If you had to multiply 327 by 829, what would you get?'
Alec: 'The wrong answer.'

Dad: 'I hope you're not talking in class any more?'
Alec: 'Not any more, just about the same amount!'

Teacher: 'How do you make sugar cubes?'
Alec: 'From square sugar beet!'

Teacher: 'I have great pleasure in giving you 90 in maths.'
Alec: 'Why don't you let your hair down. Enjoy yourself and give me 100!'

Teacher: 'If you had five chocolate bars and your friend asked for one of them, how many would you have left?'
Alec: 'Five. He can buy his own!'

Teacher: 'I'd like to go one whole day without having to scold you.'
Alec: 'Well, you have my permission.'

John: 'What's a brass band?'
Alec: 'An orchestra with no strings attached!'

George: 'Roger will never be a leader of men.'
Alec: 'I agree. But he's a great follower of women!'

'Nancy's dad is a blacksmith.'
  'Is that why she's forging ahead?'

'Wendy's mother is a doctor.'
  'Boy! Can she operate!'

'Sheila's only a draughtsman's daughter, but she sure knows where to draw the line.'

'Anne is an electrician's daughter.'
    'She certainly has good connections.'

Friend: 'People are using a lot of recycled paper these days.'
Alec: 'I'll get more excited about recycled paper when they can make trees out of it!'

Friend: 'My neighbour is an expert on Ancient Greece."
Alec: 'You mean she never cleans her oven!'

'Ned's the son of a fisherman.'
    'All the girls seem to swallow his line.'

'John's mum is an optician.'
    'Is that why John keeps making a spectacle of himself?'

George: 'Peter has a mechanical mind.'
Alec: 'But some of the screws are loose.'

'When he was a baby, we called him our little acorn. Now he's grown up, he's a big nut!'

'*When John goes to the zoo, he needs two tickets.*'
   'Why?'
'*One to get in and one to get out.*'

'*I hear Gary is girl crazy.*'
   'Yes, girls won't go out with him, that's why he's crazy!'

'*Do you think Peter has a big mouth?*'
   'Put it this way, he can eat a banana sideways!'

'*Jackie thinks she's a great entertainer.*'
    'That's a laugh. She couldn't entertain a doubt!'

'*Perhaps she just needs better gags.*'
    'Yes, to stop her opening her mouth!'

'*She has a waterproof voice.*'
    'What do you mean?'
'*It can't be drowned out.*'

'His family are real snobs. They have monogrammed tea bags!'

'He's a person who's going places.'
    'The sooner the better!'

'He holds people openmouthed with his conversation.'
    'Of course he does. They can't stop yawning!'

'He's a bit dull until you get to know him. After that, he's a real bore!'

Mary: 'They say that Wendy's stories always have a happy ending.'
Alec: 'Well, everyone is happy when they end!'

'George is good for people's health. When they see him coming, they take a long walk!'

'Ben is a man of few words.'
'That's right, but he keeps repeating them!'

'He's like a summer cold.'
'What do you mean?'
'You can't get rid of him!'

'He's a boring fellow, but he does have flashes of silence!'

'It's not that he doesn't know how to say nothing, he just doesn't know when!'

Henry: 'Linda is a fast speaker.'
Alec: 'I'll say! She can speak 120 words a minute, with gusts up to 200!'

Mary: 'I hear she always has to have the last word.'
Alec: 'That wouldn't be so bad if she ever reached it.'

John: 'I got a cute poodle for my little brother.'
Alec: 'I wish I could make a trade like that!'

'My girlfriend gave me a present that made my eyes pop out - a shirt with a collar two sizes too small!'

'She burned so much bread, her toaster has been declared a fire hazard!'

'Sally told me she'd cook dinner and asked what I would like. I told her a life-insurance policy!'

'Some people can cook, but don't. My sister can't cook, but does!'

'I understand the city will soon deal with air pollution.'
    'As soon as it sees its way clear!'

'Thomas Edison once said that genius is 1% inspiration and 99% perspiration!'
  'I hate to think of anyone that sweaty handling electricity!'

'My dad is really bald, but he tells everyone he just has a very wide parting!'

Shopkeeper: 'So you want a job. Do you ever tell lies?'
Alec: 'No, but I'm a quick learner!'

Judge: 'Guilty or not guilty?'
Man: 'Are there any other choices?'

Judge: 'This is the tenth time I've seen you in court. I fine you 100 pounds.'
Man: 'Don't I get a discount for being a good customer?'

Auntie: 'Are you a good boy?'
Alec: 'No, I'm the kind of boy my mum doesn't want me to play with!'

Paul: 'David is a liar, a cheat and a thief!'
Alec: He's improving then!'

Auntie: 'Do you ever lie?'
Alec: 'Let's just say my memory exaggerates!'

Dad: 'Why don't you play cards with Billy any more?'
Alec: 'Would you play with someone who cheats?'
Dad: 'No.'
Alec: 'Neither will Billy!'

Teacher: 'I wish you would pay a little attention.'
Alec: 'I'm paying as little as possible.'

Teacher: 'Don't whistle while you're studying.'
Alec: 'I'm not studying, just whistling!'

Teacher: 'I'm expelling you from class!'
Alec: 'No you're not. I resign!'

Teacher: 'If I had ten flies on my desk and swatted one, how many would be left?'
Alec: 'One - the dead one!'

Alec: 'I know how to get extra Christmas presents.'
Friend: 'How?'
Alec: 'I'm putting up a *stretch* sock!'

Mum: 'How many times do I have to tell you to stay away from the Christmas pudding?'
Alec: 'Never again, Mum. I just finished it!'

Dad: 'What did I say I would do if you didn't stay away from the Christmas pudding?'
Alec: 'My memory is as bad as yours, Dad. I can't remember either!'

Girlfriend: 'Just think, next week is Christmas, and a year ago I didn't even know you.'
Alec: 'Never mind about our past, think about my present!

Teacher: 'Where did Hitler keep his armies?'
Alec: 'Up his sleevies?'

Mum: 'Here are three bags of Christmas sweets for you and your sister.'
Alec: 'It's difficult to divide three, so I'll keep one and divide the other two!'

Alec: 'I wish you'd sing only Christmas carols.'
Sister: 'Why?'
Alec: 'Then I'd only have to listen to you once a year!'

Alec: 'You have to believe in Father Christmas.'
Little brother: 'Why?'
Alec: 'Otherwise, we're all being good for no reason!'

Henry: 'I'm going to give my dad a cordless shaver for Christmas.'
Alec: 'I think that's called 'course sandpaper'!'

Alec: 'I'm going to give you a teapot for Christmas.'
Mum: 'But I already have one.'
Alec: 'No you don't, I just dropped it!'

Alec walked into a sweet shop and asked the shop assistant to wrap up a small sweet for him.

'A surprise for your little sister for Christmas?'

'It certainly will be. She thinks I'm giving her a big doll!'

Teacher: 'If your dad earned ten thousand pounds a week and gave your mum half, what would she have?'
Alec: 'Heart failure!'

Teacher: 'Did you know Christopher Columbus discovered America?'
Alec: 'I didn't even know it was lost!'

Alec: 'Remember you said you'd give me ten pounds if I passed my maths exam?'
Dad: 'Yes, I do.'
Alec: 'You've just saved yourself ten pounds!'

Mum: 'What does this F mean on your report?'
Alec: 'Fantastic!'

Big sister: 'We ought to all help with cleaning up the environment.'
Alec: 'I agree. You could start by cleaning my bedroom!'

'My brother's room is so dirty - even the cockroaches have left!'